The La Cinquantaine for Violin

Practice Edition

A Learn Violin Practically Book

La Cinquantaine by Jean Gabriel-Marie

Exercises and Study Notes by Cassia Harvey

Duet by Myanna Harvey

CHP429

©2022 C. Harvey Publications
All Rights Reserved.
www.charveypublications.com - print books
www.learnstrings.com - downloadable books
www.harveystringarrangements.com - chamber music

Table of Contents

Section	Page

What's In the Book.................................... 3

How to Practice Using This Edition.................... 4

Understanding Symbols and Terms.................... 5

Reading and Playing in 3rd Position.................... 6

Getting Ready for La Cinquantaine................. 7

La Cinquantaine - Preparatory Exercises............. 8

La Cinquantaine With Study Notes.................... 17

La Cinquantaine - Performance Edition........... 20

La Cinquantaine - Violin Duet Score................ 22

La Cinquantaine - Violin II Part..................... 26

La Cinquantaine - Piano Accompaniment.............. 28

Violin Curriculum Segments......................... 32

What's In a Practice Edition

How to Practice Using This Edition
These pages have ideas for developing a practice strategy to learn the piece. From explanations of symbols and terms to beginning exercises for third position, these pages tell you how the book can be most helpful to you.

Preparatory Exercises
The most difficult parts in the piece were identified and then broken down and taught in these pages. The Preparatory Exercises are followed by *La Cinquantaine with Study Notes*.

Piece With Study Notes
La Cinquantaine is written with notes for study, including marked positions, some beat marks, and finger spacing reminders. These notes can help students practice better when they are on their own.

Complete Piece
The entire violin part to the piece is here without study notes, for performance.

Piece with Violin Duet Part
La Cinquantaine is included with a violin duet part that will allow you to practice or perform the piece with your teacher or with another violinist. If you'd like to perform the duet, the Violin II part is included by itself, after the score, so page turns can be easier.

Piano Accompaniment
The piano accompaniment is included for study, practice, or performance.

Violin Curriculum Segment - Where to Place the Piece
These pages show how *La Cinquantaine* can fit in a violin curriculum, along with recommended methods, etudes, and supplemental study books.

How to Practice Using This Edition

1. Play and master the **Preparatory Exercises** for each movement.

2. You may also, at the same time, practice the piece using **La Cinquantaine with Study Notes** (follows the Preparatory Exercises.)

3. Once you have learned the piece fairly well, you can transition to **La Cinquantaine for Performance** (page 20.)

4. Play the **La Cinquantaine Duet** part with your teacher or with another violinist.

6. If you know a pianist, play the piece with the included **Piano Accompaniment**.

7. See what to play next in a typical violin curriculum, using the lists at the end of the book.

Play-Along Sound Files

Some free Play-Along Sound Files for this book can be found at https://soundcloud.com/charveypublications/sets/lacinquantaineviolin

The files are listed according to their page in the book. They can be played online or downloaded to your device for playback at a later time.

Soundcloud can be accessed on your computer or on your mobile device, via their free app.

Understanding Symbols and Terms

In this book, **Roman Numerals** indicate strings (never positions.)
I = E string, II = A string, III = D string, IV = G string

> In the La Cinquantaine with Study Notes, subdivided beats are often indicated by small notes above the regular notes.

Positions are indicated by numbers and words: 3rd position, 1st position, etc. A line or bracket after the listed position tells you to stay in that position.

> **Arrows** are sometimes used to indicate when a finger needs to be low or high.

Metronome markings are included in the parts for both study and performance tempos. They are listed as a range (i.e. from 40-60). When you have learned the notes and bowings fairly well, you might want to start playing with the metronome and you can start at the lower end of the **study tempo**. As you progress, move the metronome up one or two notches and keep practicing. Continue getting faster until you reach the **performance tempo** where you feel most comfortable.

These markings are only approximate; feel free to play the piece at a slower or faster tempo!

Practice Tempo: ♩=40-60 (♪=80-120)

Performance Tempo: ♩=63-80 (♪=126-160)

Reading and Playing in 3rd Position

La Cinquantaine is a good piece to use to work on 3rd position. Here are a few introductory studies for the 3rd position notes used in the piece:

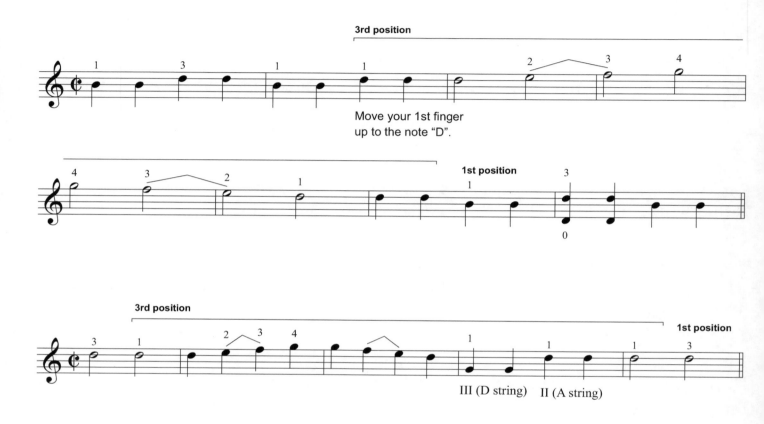

Move your 1st finger
up to the note "D".

Shifting to 3rd position across strings:

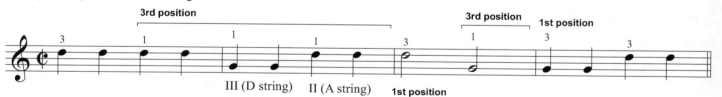

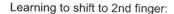

Learning to shift to 2nd finger:

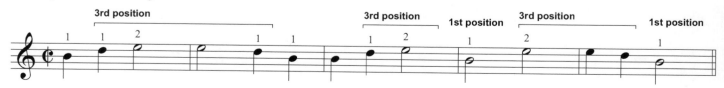

Getting Ready for La Cinquantaine

Prerequisite Skills

- Basic ability to shift to and play in 3rd position.
- Ability to play staccato (hooked bowing.)
- Ability to play two octave A minor and A major scales.

A Minor Scale (Natural Minor) and Arpeggio:

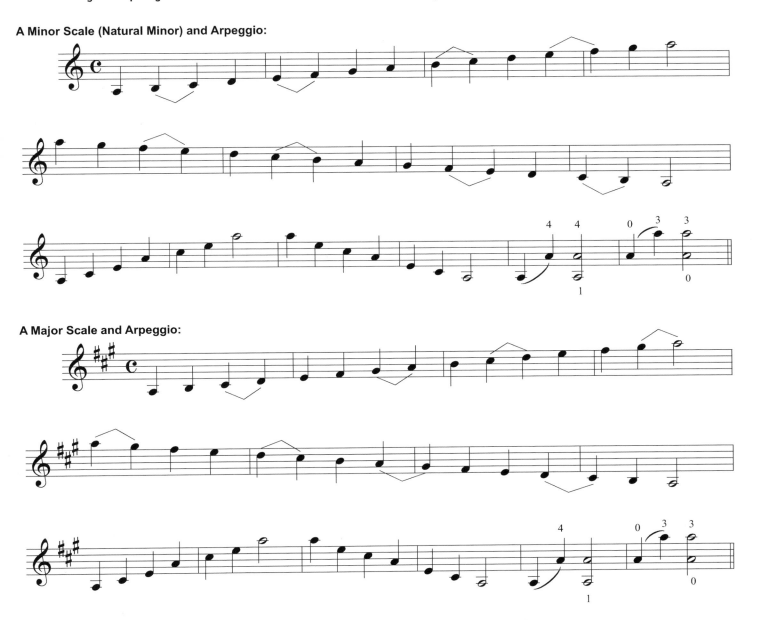

A Major Scale and Arpeggio:

Recommended Books to Study Before or Along With *La Cinquantaine*

- Finger Exercises for the Violin, Book One (CHP185)
- Third Position for the Violin (CHP196)
- Third Position Study Book for the Violin (CHP217)
- The Two Octaves Book for Violin (CHP265)

1. Shifting to Third Position
Measures 1-2

2. Shifting and Grace Notes
Measures 1-4

Grace notes are small notes that are played very quickly before the note that follows.

3. Learning to Move the Fingers Quickly
Measures 1-4

4. Learning the Notes in Third Position
Measures 1-4

5. Learning to Play the "A" Harmonic: Measures 4-5

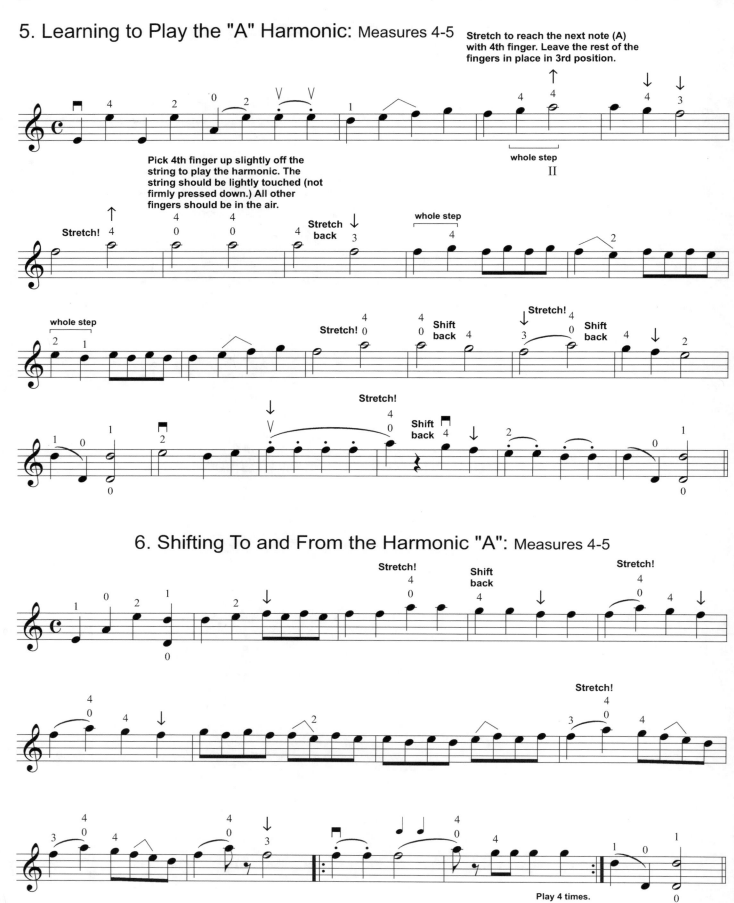

Stretch to reach the next note (A) with 4th finger. Leave the rest of the fingers in place in 3rd position.

Pick 4th finger up slightly off the string to play the harmonic. The string should be lightly touched (not firmly pressed down.) All other fingers should be in the air.

6. Shifting To and From the Harmonic "A": Measures 4-5

Play 4 times.

7. Shifting Back to Low 2nd Finger
Measures 4-6

8. The Trill Motion
Measures 7, 15, 39, etc.

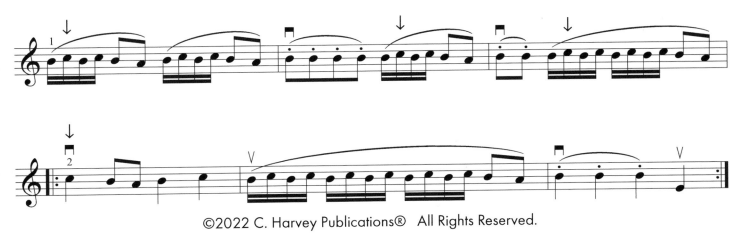

9. How to Trill
Measures 7, 15, 39, etc.

10. Counting While Trilling
Measures 7, 15, 39,etc.

11. Shifting To and From Matching Notes
Measures 15-19

12. Third Position Intonation: Measures 21-24

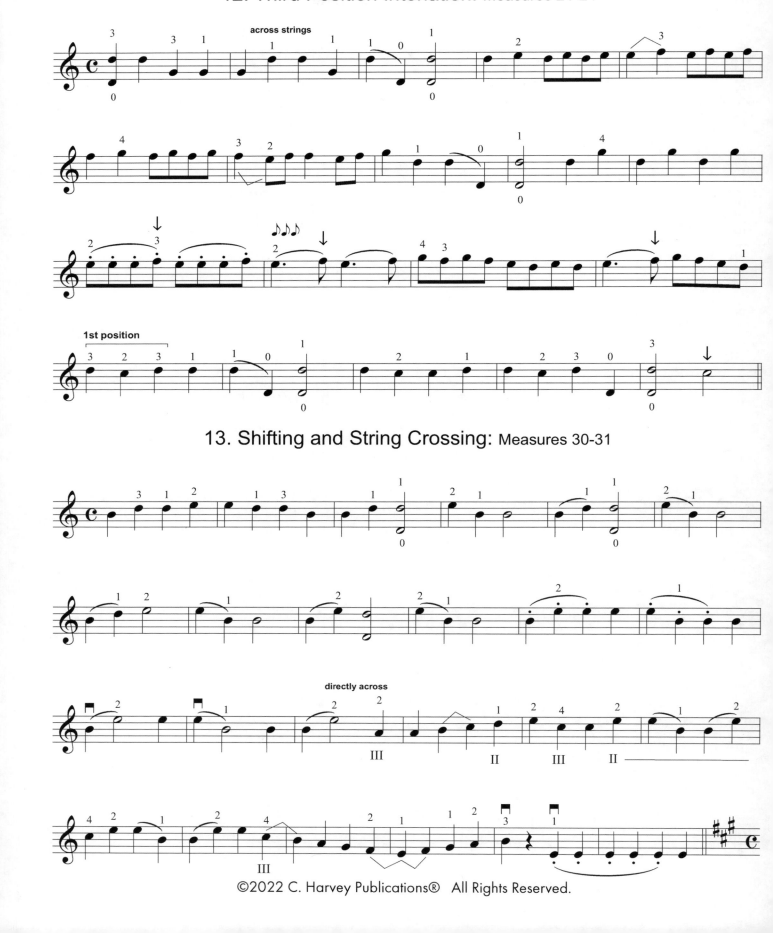

13. Shifting and String Crossing: Measures 30-31

14. Playing in A Major
Measures 41-66

15. Playing on the Lower Strings in A Major
Measures 41-66

16. Crossing Strings to High 3rd Finger
Measures 41-57

17. Bowing
Measures 45, 48, 60, 62

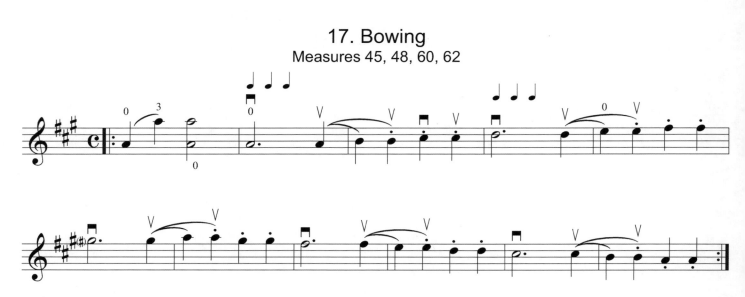

18. High 3rd Finger Twister
Measures 50, 56-57, 63

La Cinquantaine With Study Notes

Gabriel-Marie
Edited by C. & M. Harvey

I = E string   III = D string
II = A string   IV = G string

Andantino: Moderately, slightly faster than Andante

Practice Tempo: ♩=40-60 (♩=80-120)

sotto voce: a dramatic lowering of volume; hushed.

cresc.: increase the sound

sotto voce: a dramatic lowering of volume; hushed.

cresc.: increase the sound

rit.: gradually get slower

a tempo: resume normal speed

La Cinquantaine: Performance Part

Gabriel-Marie
Edited by C. Harvey

Andantino

Performance Tempo: ♩=63-80 (♩=126-160)

La Cinquantaine - Duet

Piece by Gabriel-Marie
Duet by M. Harvey

This page is left blank for page turns.

La Cinquantaine - Violin II

Piece by Gabriel-Marie
Duet by M. Harvey

Andantino

La Cinquantaine - Piano Accompaniment

Gabriel-Marie
Edited by Myanna Harvey

Violin Curriculum Segments
When to Use *La Cinquantaine* in a Course of Study

Step One: Beginning Level

Methods
- Learning the Violin, Books One (CHP280) and Two (CHP285)
- String Builder, Book One (published Belwin)
- Essential Elements for Violin, Book One or Essential Elements 2000 for Violin (published Hal Leonard)
- Suzuki Book One (if using a modified Suzuki approach) (published Summy-Birchard)

Exercises
- The Open-String Book for Violin (CHP249)
- Early Exercises for Violin (CHP183)
- Learning the Notes on the Violin series, Books 1-4 (CHP424, 425, 426, 427)
- Knowing the Notes for Violin (CHP132)
- I Can Read Music, by Martin (published Summy-Birchard)

Supplements and Etudes
- Playing the Violin, Book One (CHP298)
- Beginning Fiddle Duets for Two Violins, by M. Harvey (CHP303)
- The Blackberry Blossom Fiddle Book for Violin, by M. Harvey (CHP383)

Repertoire Books
- Stepping Stones for Violin (published Boosey & Hawkes)
- Waggon Wheels for Violin (published Boosey & Hawkes)
- Easy Solos for Beginning Violin (published Mel Bay)
- The Student Violinist: Bach (published Mel Bay)
- Violin Recital Album, First Position, Volume 1, by Sassmannshaus (published Bärenreiter)

Concertos/Concertinos
- Kuchler Concertino in G Major, Op. 11 (published Bosworth)

Note: Books published by C. Harvey Publications are noted with an item number (CHP101) and are available at www.charveypublications.com and/or www.learnstrings.com, as well as where you purchased this book.

Step Two: Early-Intermediate Level; More Complicated First Position

Methods
- Playing in Keys for Violin (CHP254)
- String Builder for Violin, Book Two (published Belwin)
- Essential Elements for Violin, Book Two (published Hal Leonard)
- Suzuki Books Two and Three (if using a modified Suzuki approach) (published Summy-Birchard)

Exercises
- Finger Exercises for Violin, Book One (CHP185)
- The Triplet Book for Violin, Book One (CHP267)
- First Position Scale Studies for the Violin (CHP317)
- Scales in First Position for Violin by Whistler (published Rubank)
- Double Stop Beginnings for Violin, Book One (CHP247)
- Open-String Bow Workouts for Violin, Book One (CHP352)

Supplements, Duets, and Etudes
- Playing the Violin, Book Two (CHP324)
- First Etude Album for Violin, by Whistler/Hummel (published Rubank)
- 60 Studies, Op. 45, Book One, by Wohlfahrt (published Schirmer or Carl Fischer)
- Flying Fiddle Duets for Two Violins, Book One (CHP263) and Book Two (CHP307), by M. Harvey
- Flying Solo Violin, Book One, by M. Harvey (CHP400)

Repertoire Books and Solo Pieces
- Solo Time for Strings, Book Three, by Etling (published Alfred)
- Solos for Young Violinists, Book One, by Barber (first half of book) (published Alfred)
- Violin Recital Album, First Position, Volume 2, by Sassmannshaus (published Baerenreiter)
- Kreisler *Chanson Louis VIII & Pavane* (published Carl Fischer)

Concertos/Concertinos (in approximate order of study)
- Rieding Concerto in B Minor, Op. 35 Practice Edition (CHP365)
- Seitz Concerto No. 2 (published Bosworth or Schirmer)
- Seitz Concerto No. 5 (published Bosworth or Schirmer)

Note: Books published by C. Harvey Publications are noted with an item number (CHP101) and are available at www.charveypublications.com and/or www.learnstrings.com, as well as where you purchased this book.

Step Three: Intermediate Level; Starting Third Position

Methods
- Third Position for the Violin (CHP196)
- Suzuki Books Three, Four (if using a modified Suzuki approach) (published Summy-Birchard)
- Introducing the Positions, Vol. One, by Whistler (published Rubank)

Exercises
- Finger Exercises for Violin, Book Two (first position) (CHP266)
- Double Stop Beginnings for Violin, Book Two (first position) (CHP248)
- Third Position Study Book for the Violin (CHP217)
- The Two Octaves Book for Violin (CHP265)

Supplements and Etudes
- 60 Studies, Op. 45, Book Two, by Wohlfahrt (published Schirmer or Carl Fischer)
- Fiddles on the Bandstand; Fun Duets for Two Violins by M. Harvey (CHP367)

Repertoire Books
- Solo Time for Strings, Book Four, by Etling (published Alfred)
- Solos for Young Violinists, Book One, by Barber (last half of book) (published Alfred)
- Flying Solo Violin, Book Two, by M. Harvey (CHP403)

Short Pieces
- **Gabriel-Marie La Cinquantaine Practice Edition (this piece)**
- Fiocco *Allegro* (published International or Schott)
- Portnoff *Russian Fantasia* (published Carl Fischer)

Concertos/Concertinos (in approximate order of study)
- Kuchler Concertino in D Major, Op. 15 (published Bosworth)
- Ruegger Concertante in G Major (published Carl Fischer)
- Vivaldi Concerto in G Major, RV310m, Op. 3, no. 3 (published Schott or Edition Hug)

Note: Books published by C. Harvey Publications are noted with an item number (CHP101) and are available at www.charveypublications.com and/or www.learnstrings.com, as well as where you purchased this book.

Step Four: Late-Intermediate Level; Learning Other Positions

Methods
- Second Position for the Violin (CHP253)
- Fourth Position for the Violin (CHP246)
- Suzuki Book Five (if using a modified Suzuki approach) (published Summy-Birchard)
- Introducing the Positions, Vol. Two, by Whistler (published Rubank)

Exercises
- G Major Shifting for the Violin (CHP257)
- Serial Shifting for the Violin (CHP195)
- Octaves for the Violin, Book One (CHP166)
- Scale Studies (One String) for the Violin, Part One (CHP178)
- Three-Octave Scales for the Violin (CHP354)
- Shifting in Keys for Violin (CHP256)

Supplements and Etudes
- Classical Syncs: Duets for Two Violins (CHP320)
- 6 Canonic Sonatas for Two Violins, by Telemann (published International)
- Six Petits Duos, Op. 48 by Pleyel (published Schirmer)
- Etudes Speciales, Op. 36, Book 1, by Mazas (published Schirmer)
- 42 Studies for Violin, by Kreutzer (published Schirmer, International, and others)

Short Pieces
- Kreisler *Sicilienne and Rigaudon* (published Carl Fischer)
- Solos for Young Violinists, Book Two, by Barber (published Alfred)
- Solos for the Violin Player by Gingold (published Schirmer)

Sonatas/Concertos (in approximate order of study)
- Vivaldi Concerto in A Minor, Op. 3, No. 6 (published International)
- Rieding Concertino in A Minor, Op. 21 (published Bosworth)
- Handel Sonatas No. 3, 4 (published Schirmer or Carl Fischer)
- The Bach Double Violin Concerto Study Book, Vol. One (CHP342)
- Bach Concerto in A Minor (published Schirmer, International, and others)

Note: Books published by C. Harvey Publications are noted with an item number (CHP101) and are available at www.charveypublications.com and/or www.learnstrings.com, as well as where you purchased this book.

If You Find the La Cinquantaine Practice Edition Helpful, Check Out the Rieding Violin Concerto in B Minor Practice Edition!

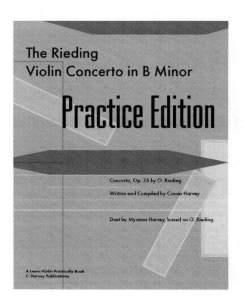

- Preparatory exercises for each difficult spot
- Entire Concerto with marked study notes including finger spacing, rhythms, and more.
- Newly written violin duet part!
- Performance copy of the solo part
- Piano accompaniment
- FREE Play-Along Tracks on Soundcloud at https://soundcloud.com/charveypublications/sets/riedingviolinbminor
- An overview of how the Concerto can be used within a structured violin curriculum

Available in print from www.charveypublications, Amazon, & other sheet music stores. Available as a PDF downloadable ebook from www.learnstrings.com. CHP365

12611772R00022